LOVE IS A CHOICE

You alone can make Love happen and why

HARRY BENSON

Table of contents

INTRODUCTION

Don't think you have to wait until you fall in love to find your happy ending. Love is a choice you can make or ignore. Ever since I started getting into mature relationships, I've been under the impression that love is a choice. I make sacrifices. I agree to compromise. I know when to back down in battle. But I also refused to give in to the demands. I rejected any contradiction to my beliefs. I looked down on everything less than I thought I deserved. So I asked myself, "Did I really choose to be in love?" The answer is yes and no. Yes, because some people they were willing to do anything to stay in love. No, because there were other people who didn't give the same chance when it came to love. Meanwhile, those who couldn't be with me also made choices. You didn't choose to work on loving me. And I couldn't blame them. We follow our intuition and jump off when our intuition says no. But should we really follow our intuition? Unfortunately, intuition doesn't always work when you're already in a relationship...but what works is the choice you make after committing to someone.

Love is a decision you make, not a gut feeling you always follow.

CHAPTER ONE
Why do people choose to fall in love?

I once asked a friend, "Why did you decide to date your current boyfriend? Is he the 'one' you've been looking for all along?" So I was surprised by her answer. She said:

"I don't know if he's right, but I'm in a mature relationship now. I chose to work on things I didn't like in this relationship, and I expect the same from him. It wasn't an overwhelming revelation, but it was enough to make me reconsider the choices I've made in the past. I dated a guy I really liked, but there were parts I didn't like so I ended the relationship. What was wrong with the one I didn't choose? Not really.

There is nothing. The fact
that I dated them
indicated that I was
attracted to them.
Unfortunately, there was
always something that
made me rethink my
future with them.
Sometimes it was the
little things that I didn't
understand, like
personality traits, and the
huge ones, like the
inherent clash of morals

and values. Basically,
most of my budding
relationships have failed.

CHAPTER TWO

Why do contract-breakers influence our decisions to fall in love?

When it comes to dating, we talk about deal breakers as if we were discussing abusive tendencies, bigoted mindsets, or obnoxious personalities. They are considered violators. For example height. I don't want to date a tall girl or a short guy... Another thing is my career. I don't want to date someone who earns less or more. Family background. I don't want to date someone who wasn't raised the same way I was. Political decision. I don't want to date someone who believes differently than I do. Religious differences. I don't want to date someone who prays to be different than you. They are all viewed as contract-breakers by some. But what we call deal-breaking is just an excuse that frees us from the choice of falling in love with someone. People have no choice when it comes to their appearance, but how they treat others. You have a choice as to which. That's what a relationship is for, right? How will your future partner handle the rest of your life? Deal breakers don't determine your future. We believe that love is a choice, and we define it by refining what's out there and working together to solve the problems that arise.

CHAPTER THREE

How can you choose to be in love?

If you're the one researching how to build the perfect relationship, you're Googling the wrong keywords, you need to find a way to build a good relationship. Perfection is subjective, but the quality of your relationship is measurable. You can see it getting better every day.

You can know if things are going in the right direction. You know when you have an unsolvable problem. You have the opportunity to decide if it's right or wrong. Voting is not just about agreeing with everything. It is only when you take the time to fully understand a person that you decide who to love, how to love, what parts to love, and why to love someone. Don't pick people because they are exactly what you want. They choose what hurts them, what upsets their minds, what makes them feel guilty, what makes them bad, what makes them good, and what makes them human. Because I know there are Nevertheless you decide to stay. They choose to be better for each other. You

choose to love each other
despite your
shortcomings, mistakes,
past, and even future
possibilities.

CHAPTER FOUR
Where do I start?

You have the tools you need to facilitate your choices: communication, honesty, and trust. If you refuse to use these tools, you are more likely to fail in your relationships.

Communicate your needs

For one thing, most people have poor reading comprehension, which makes communication very necessary. If your partner fails to meet your expectations, you are more likely to draw negative conclusions and cause problems in the relationship. Instead of sharing your observations and seeking validation, you end up thinking the worst and convincing yourself that it's time to end the relationship. Talk about what you want and what you need.

When you fall in love for the first time, you believe that person can do nothing wrong. And when they destroy your perception with flaws and weaknesses, all hell breaks loose. You lose trust that no one has helped you, and you refuse to believe they can make amends for the destruction of your ideal relationship image.

Be honest about what you want

Finally, honesty should not be limited to telling the truth when questioned. Honesty in relationships means being open about what you want instead of expecting someone to read your mind. That's why implicit rules don't work. Saying your partner should do this or that is like saying the Sun should have tea with the Moon. It would be better to simply ask, "Would you like it?" This is a more open and engaging approach to honest communication in relationships.

CHAPTER FIVE
Conclusion

You really have all the resources you need to make a decision that will make or break your relationship. No. Keep your mind alive with the choice and do your best to keep the flame alive.

www.ingramcontent.com/pod-product-compliance
Lightning Source LLC
Chambersburg PA
CBHW071251140726
47996CB00007B/2830